GLOWETIC

SHEA JETHEL

Published in USA by Trinity Publishing Company
ISBN: 979-8-9896614-3-5
Book Cover Design by Paul Nomshan
Editing by Trinity Publishing Company

Interior Layout and Formatting by Trinity Publishing Company

Dedication

Although I've been writing my whole life, I want to officially dedicate my first book to my mama. You are my earth and my foundation. I know you've always had a knack for writing as well. Remember when I stole your journal? Fun times:) I love you so much, Mom.

And to my 'Bean,' thank you to my Bean. I call you Bean because you shot up like a beanstalk. You are gorgeous, statuesque, and fearless. Every day, you grow, and because of you, I've also grown. You are my legacy and my reason. Everything I do is always for you. You are my world, Eden.

I find more things to love about you both every day. I genuinely want to thank you both for allowing me to be myself and for all of your love and support on my good and not-so-good days, but especially the not-so-good. I'm blessed to have you both in my life, and I could never express that enough.

Abba, Jesus, and Jehovah Jireh. I want to thank you for the amazing gifts that you have given me and for the ability to realize and utilize my purpose. You are the author of my life.

Nyshea

Preface

Glowetic is a book of poetry that contains memories from the 1990s and early 2000s. Memories from the author's upbringing on the outskirts of Detroit and South New Jersey carry special nostalgia for her and so many others. The poems in Glowetic capture the essence of growing up in a vibrant and diverse community filled with moments of joy, heartbreak, and self-discovery. Each verse transports readers back to a time when CD players and house phones were the norm, evoking a sense of longing for simpler days while celebrating the unique experiences that shaped her youth.

Although these poems are from personal experience, they also resonate with a wider audience as they explore universal themes of love, loss, and the bittersweet passage of time. The vivid imagery and heartfelt emotions expressed in Glowetic allow readers to not only connect with the author's memories but also reflect on their own journey through life. Whether you grew up in the 1990s or early 2000s or not, this collection of poetry invites you to step into a world where nostalgia intertwines with introspection, leaving you with a renewed perspective of how the times were and how they have shaped who you are today. Each poem in Glowetic is a snapshot of a moment in time, capturing the essence of youth and the complexities of growing up.

Through the author's words, you will be transported back to a time when life seemed simpler yet filled with profound meaning. This collection is a testament to the power of poetry to evoke emotions and provoke thought, making it a must-read for anyone seeking to reconnect with their own past and embrace the beauty of nostalgia.

Table of Contents

GLOWETIC

What are you going to do with these dreams?

It feels like success has been pursuing me.

Lately, it feels like there should be two of me.

Looking in the mirror like, Girl, it's just you and me, but I know that it is really not because I'm a always need God.

I just need to beat these odds. I'm a single black female with a story to tell.

Cards stacked against me, but still got a chance to excel.

I can't take no credit for what God allowed to be Glowetic.

He put some of the dopest and strongest women in my life.

Encouraging me and pushing me to always shine bright.

Either lending me their strength and wisdom throughout these years or something just as simple as a listening ear.

A many of thanks to all my teachers and council. Hardly think I could have done any of it without y'all.

It's time to put in this work, so cheers to a beautiful outcome!

MAGIC HOSE

Back when I was a little girl, I'd play outside all day with my friends. When I got thirsty, I never went in.

I'd just walk right over to this old green hose, and for some strange reason, that water was always deliciously cold.

That had to be the tastiest water ever. I bet it flowed right down from heaven.

Why stop our amazing play times? This water tasted, oh, so sublime.

Sometimes, I remember how the water would get stuck in that old green hose, then it would come out fast and squirt right up my nose.

Our backyard water had such a magical taste. No Kool-Aid or soda could ever take its place. Back when we had no worries, no cares, or woes.

My friends and I took turns drinking from that old green hose.

That water was thick, crisp, delicious, and clean.

If you ever drink from that old green hose, then you know just what I mean.

If you listen in real, real close, I'll tell you a secret that nobody knows. Even as an adult, every now and then I sneak a sip from that old green hose.

LETTERS TO MY YOUNGER SELF

Pimples or acne. Baby Girl, those clear up. Please cheer up. Baby, you are beautiful. Always remember that you are loved.

It's not the outer appearance that will define you.

If you ever forget, I'll always be here to remind you.

Plus, those same dudes that's ducking you now will be trying to find you.

I'm talking like in the daytime with a flashlight.

Plenty of dudes gonna try to holler when you pass by.

Forget about the people making comments on your body.

They too have self-esteem issues underlying.

It's always the ones trying to tear down others that have their own demons they are fighting.

Be careful who you call "friend."

Some of the people in your circle really ride for you, but there are plenty who just pretend.

They probably won't make it to the very end.

They just love the attention and what you can do for them. Still wondering if they are a true friend? They'll be loyal and supportive. Always clap for you when you win, and never laugh at your misfortune.

Lighten up because everything isn't do or die, and no, it isn't the world against you and I.

You were born a hard worker, so make sure you leave time for play. You are on the right path, and you will be very proud of who you are one day.

JERSEY GIRL

Don't ever let them tell you that you are just a Jersey Girl.

You are and have always been more than worthy, girl.

Making the best out of life. Living in this crazy world.

Every season is your winning season. You're still rockin' those gold door-knocker earrings for a reason.

Just like the opportunities knocking at your door.

Success is the new wave, but this ain't no Jersey Shore.

Inner voice saying, Kill it, girl. Make sure you get it, girl.

Reminds me of my sisters I grew up with back in Mt. Holly and Boro.

Gotta make sure I "Get it while it's hot."

Kinda something like an " Around the Way Girl" or a "Jenny From The Block."

Now they think I'm acting seditty like I ain't used to Millie Rock or be outside over on broad and high waiting at the bus stop.

Child, please. I thought I was gonna lose my mind back when I used to ride the river line.

Now I'm going after everything and claiming it as mine.

Best believe that I got stories to tell. Back in the day, memories about me with a pair of timbs on and some long acrylic nails.

LITTLE SISTER

My Big Sister reminded me of Laura Winslow. Back then, in my eyes, she could do no wrong.

She was so pretty and so cool. Admired by many of dudes and one of the most popular girls at school.

We were night and day, but she always knew exactly what to say.

She taught me how to be confident and take up for myself.

She would comb my hair really pretty and paint my nails.

She walked me to school and picked me up at the end of the day.

To me, my sister was just everything.

Although she was misunderstood by our parents and forced to take me everywhere, she went, I still loved her like no other.

I even thought of her as my Second Mother.

She was just shy of being 7 years older than me, so just like her is what I wanted to be.

At least, until she got pregnant at fifteen with my niece. I was never one to judge her because I knew no matter what, that I would always love her.

She moved out to start a brand-new life. First, she became a mother, then she became someone's wife.

Soon after, adulthood quickly hit her, and I began to deeply miss her. I longed for the simple days when her only title was just "My Big Sister."

WEIRD FLEX

Grew up thinking I'll probably never fit in.

Like, how many black girls you know get excited about History or watching "Hamilton?"

If they really even knew the half, I'd probably never stop getting dragged.

It's actually kind of sad. Like, I can't enjoy certain things and still be black?

Can't believe it caused me so much tension and even created some friction because I got the nerve to enunciate and use proper diction.

Damn, I can't use big words?

Guess it's not cool for us to be nerds.

Do you even hear yourself? That really sounds absurd.

Like I swear we got to be the only culture to do this.

Always felt like I had to be savage or play stupid to fit in with most of the cool kids.

Welp, I guess it's a good thing that I am more of a loner.

I'm free-spirited, and I like to keep my options open.

Respectfully, thanks for the offer to be a part of your circle.

I'd very much rather be myself and walk in my purpose.

See, if I have to give up everything I love and be someone else, then it just isn't worth it!

BLYKE ENUFF

You talk like a "White Girl!"

Oh really!?! I didn't know a person could actually sound like a color.

Not sure how that happened when I grew up in a house with just mostly me and my "very black" mother.

Pardon me; I should have probably said My Mother and I.

Am I Black enough now, or exactly how black would you like?

Let me stop you before this nonsense and ignorance goes any further.

It does not make you any "less black" if you speak properly and grew up in Suburbia.

No, I'm not bougee, and I am not putting on heirs.

It is your identity that's mistaken, while I am being self-aware.

You think talking or acting a certain way is attributed only to whiteness. Don't you know that God created us all in his image and likeness?

Also, we are royalty that descended from Kings and Queens.

Everything about me emulates the black excellence engrained in my genes.

HEAVEN SENT

Look at how far you have overcome in spite of.

All you ever needed was the right love.

Of course, they'll try to dim your light.

You are far too bright, Luv.

Oh, you're just so radiant. Who could have ever needed a light bulb?

Look at you and how you kill it. Everything meant to destroy you helps you be resilient.

Of course, the enemy thought it best to conceal it.

That passion and that fire that only you have. You were always born to feel it. That there is your God-given purpose, so no one can ever steal it.

Always remember, this is your life, girl, so make sure that you are living. Living so that you can live again. Don't ever, on your darkest day, doubt. Remember, you are a Queen, which means that you were born to win.

It's not so much the physical but the spirit that is within.

Beautiful, you are and forever will be heaven-sent.

Writer's Pain

I put my pain into a very pretty language.

I don't much like how it feels, but it got better when I explained it.

Consider yourself fortunate that you only read the words without experiencing the anguish.

How can I have writer's block if I'm still recovering from the shock?

Praying for a solution that would help the pain stop.

Using my troubles as my muse helps me to keep dropping my jewels.

That's how she'd end up becoming the new school's female version of Langston Hughes.

What an astonishing gift and a curse!

How could I ever write what I haven't lived first?

Wondering why she always felt things so strongly.

Whole time thinking while this hurts like hell, but it'll make a damn good poem.

Better yet, maybe even grow up to become a love song.

Never any feeling to be unaware or afraid of because they all eventually get put to paper.

Surrendering my deepest feelings, even the ones normally deemed sacred.

It's a necessary process for a Writer to be able to write.

Kind of sort-a like a Writer's Plight.

Jotting down feelings that would otherwise remain inside.

Finding healing in between each and every line.

HOPELESS ROMANTIC

I've learned that if it's too good to be true, then maybe it is indeed.

I know, for a fact, that broken hearts don't always bleed.

I heard the sound of a Dove's cry, but I never wanted to know what it felt like to let love pass me by.

I would rather endure a thousand bruises and ten thousand pains.

I won't ever live a lie and say that I won't fall in love again.

Even when love tears my very soul to pieces.

I dare not shun love because it feels as natural as breathing.

Though love has been the root cause of so much of my pain.

Love still gives me life, like the blood flowing through my veins.

While I've tried so many times to neglect it.

Love just shows right back up again; unexpected.

I know that love is the very reason for my existence.

I pray to experience it one day as a true and consecrated commitment.

I know from my own remembrance that being in love is one of life's greatest feelings.

My desire is to give and receive love that is everlasting and never-ending.

SIGNED, MS. A. KEYES

Boy, you give me Déjà Vu.

Daydreaming and thinking about all the things I'd do.

Damn, I barely know Ya.

Wondering what you smell like? Is it Bergamot, Patchouli, or another delicious aroma?

I know for a fact that you look equally amazing in both jeans and slacks.

I even like that you conceal all of your tats.

Got me wondering just where your head is at.

By the way, what part of town do you stay?

Got a lil' nervous cause I thought I might've walked past you the other day.

Must be my mind playing tricks on me. Thinking 'bout how you'd like these hips on me.

No, nope, nope, not even gone go there.

I just really, really, really want to be your friend. I don't want to rush anything, cuz I would rather wait and see how this ends.

It's just something about you that I can't put my finger on. Wondering how long this crush thing is going to linger on.

Maybe you're taking your sweet time because you already have a lady.

That's okay with me because I got so much to work on that I'm not even dating.

When I get back in the game and come off the bench. You better hope and pray that I don't get picked.

I'm just as dope as you are, so that would be an opportunity missed.

If you are half the Man that I think you are, you deserve the best either way. It would be selfish to assume that person is me. We may end up together eventually because what's meant to be will be.

Sincerely,

Ms. A. Keyes

FOREVER BAE

Yo'! I can't get you out of my head.

Ever Since the day I met you, I still can't forget the things you said.

I still remember what you wore down to your tee.

The only problem is, I don't think you're even thinking about me.

I even got that smile of yours down to a science.

If I said I wasn't feeling you hard, then I'd be lyin.'

Never thought that I'd feel this way, I swear.

I just looked up one day, and these feelings were there.

I know you think I'm too young for you, but I'm finally 18.

I am certain that you and I would make a really great team.

All you have to do is be my King and take me as your Queen.

Truth is, I always see your smile in my fantasies and your face in my daydreams.

You preoccupy my thoughts on a daily.

Until you are mine, I will be right here, waiting.

I'll always keep a special place in my heart for you that will never be taken.

MOMD

Boy, you got me singing Teddy P.

When somebody loves you back.

Sade - No Ordinary Love.

Nivea - Love is not always complicated.

Young Gunz—No Better Love.

Yet, I'm still not sure how to trust.

It's been quite a while since I had a crush.

Because the others left us both broken.

Now all we feel goes unspoken.

It's too early to tell, so we'll just keep it on our minds.

There's no denying these feelings that we have are one of a kind.

We always keep it real, but somehow, we are still frontin.'

We may not know exactly what, but we for damn sure are on to something.

You'll play it cool. I'll play it cool. Wishing that I had given you my number back when we were at school.

Back then, I was looking right past you, but now I'm looking dead at you.

Like, what you gone do?

Spotlight is on you, boo.

See, you aren't usually the type to catch my eye, but I really like you.

Even got me writing this poem. If I was from Japan, I'd write you a Haiku.

Wait, wait, wait. Please let me pump my breaks. Is this for real or just a sweet escape?

This might be too good to be true. I probably need to chill. So, you mean to tell me after all that praying, I finally met someone for real?

No more waiting, gaming, playing, and chasing?

No more saying anything, including B.S., they don't mean, just to try to slide up in between.

Could it be you? The Man of My Dreams.

No Judgement

I don't care that you have a regular job making a little bit of money.

Just shows me we can grow together, and it lets me know you're humble.

I don't care that you have two kids.

When you take care of them, it shows me that you have a big heart and truly know what love is.

I don't care that you have a "Baby Mama."

As long as things are completely over between you two. Hopefully, now you know exactly what to do.

All I can ask is that you stay true.

I could care less about your checkered past.

For your own sake, I just hope and pray that you have completely cleaned up your act.

Some may think that you are misunderstood.

My only ask of you is that you treat me good.

Doubters may say that I'm setting the bar much too low, but baby, I just need you to know,

When we are here, you and me, alone. Baby, we are in the "No Judgment Zone."

You're not perfect. I'm not perfect, but that just means that there's room for growth.

If we both get it right, then they can't tell us anything.

As long as we remain in the zone because here there is "No Judgement."

They may not like it all. That's okay, because, baby, we sure do love it!

THE NEXT TIME OUR EYES MEET

If only I had the courage to say all the things that I wanted to say. I know how much you would have been blown away.

If only you could look me in my eyes.

You'd know my cool exterior is just a disguise.

There's an indescribable fire raging down on the inside.

I wish that I could let my guard down so you could hear the sound of my thunderous heart beating.

That's right. If only you had been a mind reader.

You would know that you are the one that I needed.

It was you I wanted.

You don't know how hard I tried to contain and compose myself.

If I didn't tell you, how were you supposed to know?

Were you supposed to just guess?

Yes, you were supposed to sense that I was super impressed.

You should have known that on the inside, my heart was ready to leap from my chest!

How could you not know that you are one of the finest things that my two eyes have ever seen?

If it wasn't for my pride and being a lady, I'd confess that I wanted to have your babies.

Instead, I'll just pray to God that you tell me how much you like me the next time that our eyes meet.

DREADS LIKE FUTURE

He was like, What's your type?

I waited a moment, then I finally replied. "Guys who need me." You know the ones who tell me they wouldn't leave me then treat me like I'm too easy.

"Guys who use me."

The ones who sit me out on the curb like "Trash Day" every Tuesday.

The ones who give me the blues.

He said, "Listen, Sis. You might be a little twisted."

I said I know I'm a little different, but you don't know the things I've lived through.

I can't help that bad guys are what I am into. I know it sounds a little mental.

I know I should probably like sweet guys, like the ones who wear suits and ties. Not the ones who tell lies or try to get in between my thighs.

I think it might be far too late because I'm addicted to the ones who need me.

The ones most likely to mistreat me. You know the ones that are hard to reach and are more prone to cheating.

Mama told me that I deserved somebody halfway decent, so how come I keep attracting the ones that need me? Is it because both our hearts are broken like the pieces of a puzzle, the reason that I keep ending up getting played like a game of Ruzzle?

When he claims he loves me, I automatically know that he's lying. Wondering how I always end up crying?

Different dudes selling me the same exact B.S., but yet somehow, I always end up buying.

UNFRIEND

Hey, I found your page. Yep, I was being nosy.

You and those other girls looked awfully cozy.

Why don't you buy me things or take me out on fancy dates?

All you do is call me when it's super late.

Damn, is it that I'm not as pretty as them?

Keep it 100. What is it that I'm missing?

You always tell me how beautiful and fly I am when you see me.

Wait! What's up with all these flirtatious comments and these emojis I'm reading?

What do you mean I'm doing too much, and you think I'm likely to stalk you?

Tuh, I'll do you one better. I'm actually going to block you.

All of this is messing with my mental.

You'd be all in your feelings if I showed you what the guys in my DMs do.

You'd be sick and want to vomit if I showed you all my likes and all of my comments.

No, you're the one who is acting weird.

So, what if I met you on a site just like this?

We've been messing around for some time now.

It's been a little minute. I figured at least you'd have stopped seeking so much attention.

You got me, so what do you need with them?

Oh, you think it's funny? Okay, Bet! Unfollow and Unfriend.

LIQUOR ON HIS BREATH

How come you didn't think enough of me to link when you were in a sober state?

How come you always dial my number after about 4–5 drinks? When it's kinda late?

Could it be that you are drunk and don't want to be alone, or is it because you know that I'll most likely be home?

I want to ask you a million questions, but I don't want to be the one to kill your vibe.

They say a drunk man speaks sober thoughts, but knowing you, you'll still find a way to lie.

I should have known when I got that text.

You'd show up here with liquor on your breath.

Our small talk will be just a formality because you are about to do me savagely.

The whole time, I'm thinking this is so unfair because you're damn-near all the way gone and I'm not even halfway there.

Not even gonna lie. I really do want you, but something just doesn't sit right.

I want to mean more to you than being "the happy ending of another lit night."

Would you have called me if you could have gotten up with someone else?

Do I ever be on your mind when there's no liquor on your breath?

Liquor On Your Breath, Again

I bet on your way over here, you had plenty of time to think. Said that you'd be at my place in less than an hour.

I'm such a Strong and Independent Woman yet here I am waiting and willing to give you my mind, body, and power.

None of this seems quite right, like - How I hop up and rush to the shower just for you to show up as is.

In here smelling like some weed, funk, and liquor sour.

Don't get me wrong. I'm not saying that you're disgusting and funky. I'm just saying that you'd probably smell much better if I knew that you actually loved me.

Are you staying the night because you can barely drive or because you miss me and want to spend quality time?

I really want to tell you that binge drinking is actually bad for your health.

But I guess I probably shouldn't overstep. You'd probably only remind me that I'm not your girl.

Besides, next weekend you'll be back drunk texting then lying to someone else.

Not gonna lie, it's a part of me that feels a little stupid because every now and then I foolishly let you do this.

Just for me to have to help heal the heart hurt with prayer, time, and music.

VERY LOW MAINTENANCE

Guess I can only be mad at myself.

I never required flowers, chocolates, or even romance.

Shortly after "You Had Me At Hello," there I was, giving into your advances.

Thinking about every time I felt cheap and how you didn't have to work for anything.

All because You met me when I was at my lowest and when I felt weak.

Constantly lowering my standards for you to take full advantage.

I still, to this day, should have been your biggest challenge.

Like, are you for real?

Do you know how many men would kill to be in your shoes?

No, because all you ever do is leave me feeling more empty. I feel used and very confused.

Does it make you feel good to treat me like your own personal toy?

Do you ever stop and think, "She's a good woman. She deserves more."

Of course, you don't consider me. It's all about you and your wants and needs.

The only thing I have now is what's left of my dignity. I already shared with you that I needed way more.

My only recourse now is walking out the door.

UN-ENTANGLEMENT

You have already gotten what you wanted.

This one-sided arrangement just doesn't work for me any longer.

You'll string me along forever, as long as you are getting what you are getting.

As time passes, I become more and more smitten and even a little bitter.

I'm usually in it for the long haul, but this time, I am very much a quitter.

Finally picking up the pieces of my self-worth and finding ways to heal from the hurt.

I just can't keep being your trash when it's clear that I'm meant to be some man's treasure.

I'm off to find someone who actually wants to love me, not just use me for pleasure.

This isn't at all how I was raised.

I deserve love, romance, affection, and a little praise.

Not just a man who calls on me at night, but one who wants to spend most of his days.

You see, I'm finally moving around.

Praying away any soul ties that would normally keep me bound.

It's far too late for me to show you how to treat me.

They say however you start is how you will finish.

The only way to right my wrong is for me to end whatever you call "this."

LOVE BULLY

You are just a love bully.

I gave you my heart fully.

You played me ever so coolly.

Should have never let my emotions overrule me.

Now I can't seem to wrap my head around why you didn't want to love me down.

I needed you. Hoped that you could love me now.

When I searched for your heart, it was nowhere to be found.

Here in my heart, you are everywhere.

Question is, how can I get you out?

Please stop hurting me, because this just isn't fair.

Why am I the one with all the feelings when you don't even seem to care?

I have decided that I'm no longer going to be your victim.

I know I'll be much better once I get you completely out of my system.

REALIZATION

I finally realized. With you, there was never a safe space.

Your arms are not my safe place.

Telling me that we can still be friends.

Knowing that you only said that to save face.

Can you refund me any time that you caused me to waste or help me regain my precious days?

I really wish I never met up with you and went on a first date or drove over to your place the next day.

From my memory bank, your name is something that I long to erase, right along with the sound of your voice, telling me to stay safe.

The sheer irony of it all. As if you ever cared about my well-being.

You can save your closure.

Hindsight 20/20. It's now that I can actually see it.

These past few days I spent reflecting, I had the revelation that I needed.

GAS LIGHTER

Okay, I see you gas lighter.

If I had it to do all over again, the day that I met you I would have passed by ya.

Playing with my heart is the quickest way for you to start a mass fire.

I'm so hip to your tricks; you are such a bad liar.

If it was what you say then how come I got more questions than you got answers?

When I ask you what your truth is, you become a tiny dancer.

I don't believe in 3rd or 4th chances.

You're right I dreamed it all up.

Maybe you were just a deflection because I needed true love.

I see now that I can only get that from the man above.

Gas lighter, pass me your lighter so that I can burn what's left of my feelings up.

Gotta burn this right out of me.

Set ablaze any doubt that may be left in me.

Doubt that I may not be worthy. Worthy of a love both certain and deserving.

Worthy of a love that would help me fulfill my God-given purpose.

So here, catch!

I'm gonna toss you your lighter back.

By the way, about that last text that I sent you.

No need for you to even reply to that.

HEARTBREAKER

When I kissed you, I really meant it.

If you needed my last, on you I would have spent it.

I gave you my heart, and you regifted it.

What did I do to you? This time, would you please be specific?

Visions of you and the first night we met replay in my head like a matinee.

Honestly, sometimes it still feels like just yesterday.

I'd never tell you, but sometimes, when I close my eyes, I can still smell you.

I try to tell myself all the time that it was never love, just lust.

Might've been that for you, but as for me, that's completely untrue.

I was in deep infatuation and awe of you.

It was the first time I ever felt the wind get knocked out of me.

First time, I felt like I couldn't breathe.

Seems like I've been holding my breath since that very day.

Knowing deep down that you were never meant to stay.

NARCISSISTIC

You're so vain. I bet you think all my poems are about you.

Guess I'll be moving on without you.

I'm the one who puts you on a pedestal, and that's about as much as you'll ever amount to.

You know what? You're right. I probably shouldn't have even said that.

But can I please get my heart and my head back?

Definitely played me like a drum or a guitar.

If you didn't want me. How did we get this far?

Honestly, part of me thinks that you just might be pure evil.

Using me as a way to stroke your huge ego.

Now I'm thinking everything was a lie.

Next time you find someone like me, do yourself a favor and walk on by.

I cried so many tears that I'm certain I could fill up an entire jar.

I used to be love-blind, but now I see you for exactly who you are.

CHALLENGE

I should warn you that my heart has been changed.

It happened because I kept getting gamed and kept getting played.

Been hurt too many times to count, and I won't dare let it happen again.

Please pardon me if I shut you out and refuse to let you in.

Even still, if I said I wasn't feeling you, then I'd be lying.

It's not that I don't trust you. It's just that I've done enough crying.

I was wondering, maybe. Just maybe you could be the one who holds the key.

The one who cares enough to set my wounded heart free.

Then again, I just don't know, so I'm thinking that we should take it slow.

I really don't mean to sound distrustful and make you feel like a suspect.

It's just that it's been really hard finding someone with whom I can connect.

When it's all said and done, I still have a heart to protect.

If my walls are too high for you to climb, I'll understand, and I'll be just fine.

I'd rather know now before either of us waste our valuable time.

Let me know if I'm simply too much for you to handle. I'm a highly coveted prize.

Question is, Are you up for the challenge?

VULNERABILITY

Pretend I'm a bird who was just nursed back to life.

My broken wings must once again begin to fly.

Pretend I'm a deer once blinded by the brightest of headlights.

Love, it is and has always been within me. Yet only he holds the key. Slowly, slowly, slowly, and, oh, so very steady.

I'm not quite yet ready.

Tear down my walls, and you'll earn my trust.

All these years, I spent letting my love collect dust.

Remember, slow and steady if there is to be any hope for us.

Both slow and steady are an absolute must.

Promise that you will become my best friend first.

I can't take one more bad romance; I'm still in recovery from my past hurt.

I know you didn't cause me any of this pain, so my ask is rather unfair.

What should I do when I can't help that it's still here?

I wonder if you are God's answer to my prayers.

I don't know why, but this time feels surreal, but with another heartbreak, I just cannot deal.

Slow and steady because I'm still taking my time to heal.

Glowetic   Shea Jethel

What does all this have to do with you, you ask?

My answer is I just hope you are nothing like the last.

Part of me wants you to see all of me so that I can feel free.

I'll bear it all. The good, the bad, even the ugly.

The other part is scared that I will push you away.

The absolute biggest part is afraid of what will happen if you actually stay.

FREE SPIRITED

Please don't blow my natural high. Don't shoot me down.

I want to fly, fly, fly. My place is up there in the clouds.

Please let me sail.

Don't you dare pull me down to the pits of hell.

My life. My breath is in those clouds.

Up there, I'm free. Free from worry, fears, or doubts.

Don't drown me; don't choke me.

Just let me stay there, flying and floating.

Just uplift me so I'll go the distance.

I promise not to linger in suspension.

Never again begging for permission.

I'm forging toward a new beginning.

A beginning that's up there in the clouds.

A life that's best lived freely and out loud.

Free, free, free from worries, fears, and doubts.

Joyous and courageous.

Free, free, free sort of like a bird who's never been caged in.

A bird that never had their wings clipped.

So, don't snap me back into your reality or demand that I get a grip.

My life. My breath is in those clouds. There, I'm free.

I can be me; I can dream; I can even scream!

Letting my light in the sky shine. May it beam and beautifully gleam.

Please don't shoot me out of the sky. I don't belong down below because my place is up high.

There on the ground is where I would die because the vultures would rather pick away at my eyes.

Folks will mock me in my helpless state as they pass me. Looking on, jeering, and laughing.

I'd be food for the big, ugly, black flies. I beg of you, please don't shoot. I swear that I belong there, up high in the sky. It's the only place I can breathe, where I can fly.

WHISPERS

Man, enough is enough!

I really wish all these whispers would just hush.

Last night, they told me I was doing way too much.

This morning, they said I wasn't doing enough.

I dare not ask which one it is.

All I know is that I'm plain sick of them.

On my worst days, they try to tell me that it might be better if I just end it all because I don't have a friend at all.

They tell me that I won't ever find peace or real love, so maybe I should just give up.

I have decided those whispers are just completely absurd. That's when I decided to pray and read God's holy word.

They can be so loud in my head, but I'm determined to respond back with what God says.

Who the son sets free is free indeed.

God will surely complete the work that he started in me.

I am worthy. I am chosen. Those lies will no longer break my focus.

I can and will be a new creation using God's promises as my daily affirmations.

I am more than a conqueror, which makes me both strong and courageous.

NAKED

Who told you you were naked?

Who's lies have you digested?

Who left you broken, torn, and dissected?

Who told you that you couldn't make it?

I bet it was the same one that told you you were naked.

This is not the state God left you in.

Dare not make a snake your confidant.

Perfect love does not condemn.

Who are they, and what makes them so right?

Can't you see how perfect you are in God's sight?

He said his yoke was easy and his burden is light.

I know it gets heavy holding on to the lies.

Darling, if it doesn't edify, then it's not his fruit.

It's time to let go of all the baggage you have been holding onto.

Discard the lies to embrace the truth.

You are more than a conqueror.

With God, all things are possible.

In the Book of Life, God is the author.

He's a strong tower, so trust and have faith.

His ways are not ours. When we are weak, just remember that he has all power.

You are not worthless. May the Lord grant you strength and courage. The devil is a lie.

You shall live and not die. Dry your eyes now that you've had a good cry.

You are not naked. You have everything that you'll ever need. Have faith, believe, and just breathe.

Now, tell whoever told you were naked that they are a liar.

In Jesus' name, I cancel every attack and assignment!

NEW ME. WHO DIS?

Morning by morning, new mercies I see.

Who are you to say who I can or can't be?

Even my skin sheds, and my cells, they renew.

If I want to change for the better, then that is exactly what I'll do.

I'm sorry, I may have been toxic just a short while ago.

Since then, I've been blessed with some new information and strength that helped me to grow.

Please don't pigeonhole me because you refuse to see past the old me.

I am worthy of a new start. I asked God to create in me a clean heart.

I am human, and I make a lot of mistakes.

I can become a better me and be healed through faith.

So, I'm taking this journey day by day.

Please don't call me delusional, phony, or fake.

I only made it this far through God's grace.

You are more than welcome to take the same steps if you dare.

I'll tell you the best way to get there is through prayer.

Also, you have to be willing to sacrifice your life for him.

It cost me some family and plenty of so-called friends, but you will find out it was all worth it in the end.

NECESSARY

If just one little thing had been different, maybe you wouldn't be living the life you are living.

Every minor detail was needed in the grand design.

Every struggle and every blessing beautifully and intricately intertwined.

Every setback that allowed blessings to become aligned. Apart from God's grand scheme to present the divine.

His ways are not our ways. He already knew we wouldn't have appreciated the glorious sunshine without those rainy days.

He is so detailed in his blessings that every single variable is connected.

He is the very reason every dreadful thing can still turn out better than ever expected or fathomed.

Surrendering it all to the one who has never lost a battle.

SHEDDING

Never thought I'd be happy to say that I'm a loser or that I don't know where I am going.

That's right, I am completely lost.

I'm giving it all away. I'm paying a sizable cost.

In exchange, the mask, the shame, and the pain are slowly falling off.

No, I don't know what's about to happen, and don't dare ask me where I'm headed.

All I know for sure is that I'm shedding.

It had to be this way. I am willing, and more than ready.

That ole' broke me. She no longer suits the new me.

Up and out of the miry clay is where my father uproots me.

As the author and the finisher of my faith, causing the old me to shed away.

Once Jesus calls your name and ministers his truth, sin just doesn't hit the same as it used to.

Slowly but surely, you start becoming anew.

Praying that the Holy Spirit moves through you.

Welcoming God's holy words so they can transform you.

So, when you hear it's something about you that seems different, please don't get upset or defensive.

Remember, it's probably just the shedding, the breaking, and the shifting.

My Church Girls

I'm glad God saw fit to surround me with heavy hitters.

Strong praying women that I like to call my sisters.

We pray for each other through our storms.

Always leaning on his everlasting arms.

They love me enough to keep it 1000% real.

Been here by my side, fighting on life's battlefield.

They know sometimes I get really weary.

At those moments, they validate my feelings and then help me to refocus on my vision more clearly.

They give me life, and how they uplift and encourage me in Christ.

Honey, if iron sharpens iron they must be some Ju Jitsu knives.

I don't know anyone that goes harder than these Women of God praying and laying it all at the altar.

So glad to have them in my corner. They are my sisters, and we are his daughters.

What a blessing to stand among godly wisdom and counsel!

Together, we will witness miracle after miracle and move mountain after mountain.

Father, I pray wherever my sisters are that your blessings, protection, and favor always surround them.

Keep your daughter loving, healthy and in your holy will so that we may all continue stomping on the devil in our highest heels.

Ms. Mya Angelo

Could it be so? Shea Shea la faux something like the next Maya Angelou?

Poetry flows within me.

I've always found it to be soul-cleansing.

Since 7th grade class with Mrs. Colavita.

Who knew back then? It'd be words to complete her.

Been in love since that very day. Finding a way to express all the things that mere words could never say.

Another one of my passions, who knew writing would surpass my love of fashion?

I set out to design and have my own clothing line.

Perhaps I could write as a hobby, like in my spare time.

Ha! Who knew? God, that's who.

Life is funny because, lately, baby, that is all I ever do.

I never got my designs onto a runway or into an outlet, but I only had a few limited minutes, so I went back to penning.

Actually, right now I'm writing, and it feels like I'm close to winning.

Yep, it was meant to be. Destined to be one of the greats.

Imagine Maya, Langston, and then me. Must be fate.

Wouldn't that really be something?

A black girl from Jersey was inspired by both Maya Angelou and Edgar Allen Poe.

Doing exactly what she loved based on the words that flowed from her soul.

UNAPOLOGETIC

Baby, I'm so much more than wavy.

I'm deep. I've got depth like the ocean. I'm blessed.

I'm not bragging or boasting.

I'm just saying that I'm happy that I'm chosen.

Glory and honor are my new designer clothing.

While y'all steady hating and roastin.' I've got depth.

See I know that beauty is fleeting and charm is deceitful, but my essence is much deeper.

I've always been an overachiever, favor receiver, and miracle believer.

This is nothing new to me. Proud to say that I'm not who I used to be.

Strength and dignity are my finest fine Jewelry.

I'm on a mission to succeed. I know who I am. I am a queen.

I have everything I need to create my dreams.

Everything you currently see is the fruit, while I am the tree.

God put greatness inside of me.

That doesn't mean that I will ever be perfect.

It does mean that I am finally walking into my purpose.

THE END

Acknowledgment

Man, it's definitely been one heck of a ride that is still moving, lol. I'm beyond grateful. A huge thank you to anyone who took the time to purchase and read this book. I really hope that you enjoy reading it as much as I enjoyed creating it. I hope a big smile forms whenever you are reading any of the poems and you recall your own memories and experiences.

I want to especially thank my girls, Porsha, Krystal, Valerie, Ash, Ness, and Nay. You guys have held me down with so much support and encouragement. Ashley, my "A," thank you so much for being my safe space, sounding board, and secret keeper throughout the years. I love you infinitely. Thanks for all the times you have had my back when I was deep in the trenches, Cass.

My favorite neighbor, Ms. Nadine, and my other mothers, Stacie, and Ines, thank you for being examples of strength, love, leadership, and community. Key Wesley and Kelli G, thank you both for your kindness and friendship, even when I did not know how to reciprocate. Your inner beauty and both of your hearts are just as lovely as your outward appearance—forever fine.

Thank you, B, Shay, and Mrs. Kay. You were an inspiration and an example for me to step out on faith and follow my dreams unknowingly, Mrs. Kay. I truly admire the relationship that you and Shay have as mother and daughter. You all were instrumental in my meeting, Gina.

Gina, Gina, Gina! Thank you for your accountability, assertiveness, and business savvy. Keep up the amazing work in helping others realize and maximize their potential. A sincere thank you to Dr. Joyce for helping me to find my words and put my thoughts to paper in a way that made me tear up reading my own information!

About The Poet

Shea Jethel is the vibrant new voice behind "Glowetic," her soul-stirring debut poetry collection. Residing in North Texas, she dedicates herself to honing her craft and exploring the depths of human emotions through her evocative words. With a unique blend of raw vulnerability and empowering messages, Shea's poetry captivates readers and invites them on a transformative journey of self-discovery.

Hailing from the colorful tapestry of South Jersey, Shea's verses carry the rhythm of the 90s and the heart of the early 2000s. Today, Shea's work captures that blend of unfiltered nostalgia and profound tranquility. When she's not weaving memories into her poems, you might catch Shea sharing her thoughts and insights as a weekly blogger while immersing herself in the works of other writers to further fuel her creativity. Her biggest influences are Langston Hughes, Maya Angelou, and Sistah Souljah. "Glowetic" invites you to experience the glow of memories through Shea's eyes—a true ode to the times that shaped her.

Made in the USA
Columbia, SC
11 August 2024